THE FORMULA OF BUSINESS

THE BUSINESS FORMULA

THE FORMULA OF BUSINESS

INDEX

Introduction

Chapter 1: The marketing funnel explained

Chapter 2: How the real business builder makes the most profit

Chapter 3: A "Product laucher Vs a real business builder"

Chapter 4: Pareto principle: The 80/20 rule

Chapter 5: What is the marketing funnel?

Conclusion

THE FORMULA OF BUSINESS

THE FORMULA OF BUSINESS

Introduction

Most people when they think about creating an online business think about creating a product, selling it and hope to get enough capital to finance their next product idea. This kind of thinking is short-term, and does not lend itself well to long-term business. When you stop and think of a long-term business model, whether it's online, offline or a mix of both, you really need to think about the big picture. What's really needed is a method to capture potential customers, turn them into small-time customers, and gradually turn them into customers who spend more with you in terms of three factors: frequency, monetary value, and timeliness. In terms of frequency, I think it's obvious that we want them to spend more

THE FORMULA OF BUSINESS

money on our business on a more regular basis. In terms of monetary value, we'd like every transaction to be bigger, and we'd like you to spend more per transaction. When it comes to today, ideally they should buy last week instead of five years ago. This makes them a fresher customer who is more likely to buy back soon, promoting the other two qualities I just mentioned. There is also a fourth quality that is rarely discussed. We don't necessarily care how they buy from us, only that they buy from us. However, some distribution channels are significantly cheaper than others. Ideally, then, the media, or the method you used to bring the sale, becomes increasingly important. So how do you turn a product-to-product mentality into a prosperous long-term business? Well, to begin with, you need to have a viable business model. And part of that business model should include the "marketing funnel. This is where it comes in.

Chapter 1: The marketing funnel explained

The marketing funnel is not a complicated process. It is a tool, or a process, to separate your prospects and customers into different cubes.

For example, we want to know the difference between our potential customers, customers who spend less than $10 a year with us, customers who spend more than $10,000 a year with us on a regular basis and everything else.

This allows us to focus our efforts on the

THE FORMULA OF BUSINESS

smallest group of customers who spend the most money with us. In other words, we are trying to maximize the return on investment.

In a moment we're going to take a closer look at the marketing funnel to see how it works, in addition to what you probably know as the "80/20 rule.

Because that's going to boost those customers' ROI and spend most of my money with us, those customers who spend less, and those gift seekers and those who kick tires.

Most sellers are missing at least one or two of these crucial steps that are causing them to leave on the table bundles of money that might otherwise be in their pockets.

Chapter 2: How the real business builder makes the most profit

A typical business model could focus on three areas for each transaction: Recency, frequency and monetary value.

For example, let's take a typical fast food restaurant and use it as an example. There are mainly three ways to grow a business.

1. You can acquire more customers, which is what most companies try to do.

THE FORMULA OF BUSINESS

2. You can get them to spend more with you for each transaction (monetary value).

3. And you can get them to buy from you more often (frequency).

There are other ways to deal with investments and so on, but for the sake of this discussion, keep it simple and refer to the growth of your business as building a strong customer base.

So the goal, then, becomes to call how do we do any of those three things? Ideally, we would like to do all three.

That's where your business plan should come into play.

THE FORMULA OF BUSINESS

When you think in terms of a product, you're talking about a single instance of something that can be leveraged to gain greater long-term assets through the use of this fairly simple model.

But let's get back to the fast food model.

When we talk about cross-selling, that's similar to when you ask for a sandwich and they ask, "Do you want fries with that?"

When we use the term "sell more," it's similar to that fast food restaurant that asks you, "Do you want to super-size that?

You may already know this information. But

THE FORMULA OF BUSINESS

we have to start with a frame of reference.

The real money that can be earned is in what we call the "back end".

For example, if you order something from a catalog, maybe even a small "impulse buy" item, and then mail you information so you can buy a more expensive item, that's what we call "back-end selling.

It's where the business really grows.

Many times a company will lose money on the front-end sale, so you can recoup that profit on the back-end. We call that a "loss leader.

THE FORMULA OF BUSINESS

It's what separates single-product companies that occasionally engage in single-product production from those that engage in long-term production.

And if you have long-term ambitions for your business, that's the line of thinking you need to take.

Unique sales rarely sustain a business for long. Not only that, the profits they produce are minuscule compared to companies that have a broader vision.

Let's take a closer look at why these methods are so successful, and the type of customer you really want to focus on to bring your business to the stratosphere.

Chapter 3: A "Product laucher Vs a real business builder"

What separates "product launchers" from business builders?

A product launcher thinks about what's fashionable for the next few months, and concentrates on selling a product to fill that hot, but limited need.

A business builder thinks longer-term and sells products and services that can be leveraged in the future as the situation arises.

THE FORMULA OF BUSINESS

A business builder thinks in terms of what will increase his wealth over a longer period of time. That is, how to build your business over the long term, regardless of what is fashionable at the moment.

That does not mean that a business builder will ignore what is considered hot right now. Rather it means capitalizing on that trend, but they also think about how it will transform into something else that they can be prepared to provide.

A product launcher has to constantly reinvent itself to stay on top of the current trend. Not only that, the challenges get bigger with the passage of time, and the amount of work needed to maintain a real

THE FORMULA OF BUSINESS

business becomes virtually impossible to maintain over the long term.

Also, once the initial clutter over the product launcher's product has calmed down, he will see a severe decrease in profits until eventually the web traffic, and his sales will eventually slow down to a trickle.

On the other hand, a true business builder will always see a constant flow of sales, and will look for ways to continually maximize revenue. You are not looking for money in the short term. You're in it for the long haul.

Are you starting to see a pattern here?

The real business builder is in the business of creating and growing a long-term company

THE FORMULA OF BUSINESS

that will survive the good times and the bad.

The product launcher, on the other hand, will pursue one hot trend after another until all ideas are exhausted.

Over time, what category would you like to be in?

To me, the answer is obvious.

I prefer to build a solid business base that will stand the test of time, even if it is less "sexy" than the wonders of a single short-term success that a product launcher will produce.

THE FORMULA OF BUSINESS

Now let me be frank here.

It is certainly possible to do both. That is, you can be a product launcher under several pen names, while at the same time keeping a solid business separate under your own name (or even another pen name).

It really boils down to what your goals are.

But think about this: if you were to become a product launcher, it would require a constant pulse in your market(s), much more work than you think it could be, but the good news is that occasionally you can get short term, but sometimes huge payments.

On the other hand, a true business building

THE FORMULA OF BUSINESS

model allows you the freedom to run your business as you see fit, producing constant revenue streams, and does not always require you to think of the next hottest thing.

I'm not telling you to go one way or the other. It really boils down to what your goals are, as well as your own personality and what you enjoy doing.

Chapter 4: Pareto principle: The 80/20 rule

In 1895, Italian economist Vilfredo Pareto wrote about a mathematical formula he discovered by modeling the distribution of wealth in his country and in all the other countries he studied. Pareto observed that twenty percent of the population owned eighty percent of the land. Eventually, others found similar distributions that applied to their own situations. Dr. Joseph Juran, a quality management expert who worked in the United States in the 1930s and 1940s, recognized a universal principle he called "a few vitals and many trivials.

THE FORMULA OF BUSINESS

As a result, Juran's observation that 20 percent of something is responsible for 80 percent of the results became known as the Pareto Principle, or the 80/20 Rule.

The 80/20 Rule simply means that in any situation, a few (20 percent) are vital and many (80 percent) are trivial. In other words, the 80/20 rule states that the relationship between entry and exit is rarely, if ever, balanced. In Pareto's case it meant that 20 percent of the people owned 80 percent of the wealth. In the case of Juran, he discovered that 20 percent of manufacturing defects were causing 80 percent of all problems. You can apply the 80/20 rule to almost anything.

In fact, 20 percent of your staff and colleagues probably give you 80 percent of all the support you need. Don't take them for

THE FORMULA OF BUSINESS

granted, because true advocates like them are rare. You probably read magazines and trade books, and I bet 20 percent of them contribute 80 percent of your knowledge in those subjects.

And what about those jobs at home that you wanted to do? The 80/20 Rule means that if you have a list of ten things to do, two of those things will be worth as much or more than the other eight things put together.

The 80/20 rule can be used in many ways for your business. And when I say 80/20, that's really an approximation. Sometimes it can be 70/30, sometimes 85/15, you get an idea. The crux of the matter is that a small amount of something is responsible for the vast majority of the results.

THE FORMULA OF BUSINESS

Even the way you spend your time is subject to the 80/20 Rule. Have you ever noticed that 20 percent of your efforts are responsible for 80 percent of your success? And the opposite is also true: 80 percent of your efforts are only responsible for 20 percent of your success.

Does that sound familiar?

You are in the 80 percent segment (the least desirable) of your efforts if you…

- You are working on tasks that are not your specialty.

THE FORMULA OF BUSINESS

- You are spending time on tasks that other people want you to do, but you get little or nothing in return.

- You're doing a lot of prep work that prepares you for the "real" job.

- Tasks are taking much longer than you thought.

- You often put out fires and work on "urgent" tasks.

- You're not happy, you're complaining, or you don't feel like you've accomplished your tasks.

THE FORMULA OF BUSINESS

However, you are in the 20 percent (most desirable) segment of your efforts if...

- You are outsourcing or hiring people to perform tasks outside your area of expertise or that you prefer not to perform.

- You are involved in activities that help you advance your purpose and achieve your goals.

- You are eliminating tasks quickly, especially the "core" work that needs to be done.

- You are doing things that you enjoy and feel good about.

THE FORMULA OF BUSINESS

- You may be working on tasks you don't like, but you're doing them knowing they contribute to the big picture.

- You are happy, smiling, and feel a deep sense of accomplishment in completing your tasks.

So how does the 80/20 Rule apply to the marketing funnel? And what is this funnel?

First, the 80/20 Rule. You probably know that 80 percent of your income is determined by 20 percent of your customers. If that's not the case, then you're probably missing out on many profitable opportunities. Let me explain.

THE FORMULA OF BUSINESS

If your customers contribute to your profits in a one-to-one (1:1) ratio, then that means your business model is configured in such a way that once a customer buys from you, you never sell back to them. An opportunity. A sale. End of line. It's time to move on to the next customer...

But if you continue to sell to them again and again, you will eventually discover that there are certain customers who will buy more often and spend more money with you in the long run than others. Some will keep buying once, and you'll never hear from them again. That's fine. This is going to happen no matter what system you have in place.

But your system will play an important role

THE FORMULA OF BUSINESS

in determining what those top "20 percent" will ultimately spend with you. And if you have 20 percent of the best to start with.

These people are your first customers, your first customers. They are the ones you want to treat like royalty. Just like the 20 percent of your staff and colleagues who are true advocates of your company, your "A" customers are true advocates of your company. And they show their loyalty by buying from you and referring your business to others.

Let me give you an example that illustrates how powerful references can be.

I recently started a referral program for my copywriting business. In the first two weeks

THE FORMULA OF BUSINESS

alone, they sent me more than $23,000 in new business. All for references. And that doesn't even count the joint venture partnerships in the works, where I hope the real business will come from.

Therefore, the system you want to use must have a built-in bias to encourage your customers to do so:

Make larger purchases with cross-selling and up-selling.

Shop more often.

Graduate to make purchases of larger tickets, those that give you more and greater profits.

THE FORMULA OF BUSINESS

Become an advocate for your business and refer others to you.

The system should also provide a strong incentive, an "ethical bribe," if you will, for people in your target market (i.e., your prospects) to raise their hand and become your leaders. Willingly and voluntarily.

Chapter 5: What is the marketing funnel?

Large corporations often use what is known as "open house" or brand building, advertising model, which is expensive, time-consuming and requires a lot of brand value and trust over time before people make the decision to buy from them.

With the "marketing funnel" model, a person makes a small purchase (yes, providing an email or a physical mailing address is considered a kind of payment), and over time you "funnel" your customers into more and more high-end products and services, step by step, selling them to the next level.

THE FORMULA OF BUSINESS

The two are completely different business models, and both work their way. For most entrepreneurs, however, the branding model is too costly and time-consuming to use on its own, as it involves many resources that are simply not practical. That doesn't mean you shouldn't use it within your means. In fact, you'll soon see how to incorporate both open house and funnel marketing models into your system (we're getting warmer to begin with!).

So by "channeling" (others call it "back ending" or "up-selling"-Dan Kennedy calls it "gathering the herd") your prospects to pay customers, you're paving the way to provide them with tremendous value. So much value, in fact, that your customers begin to expect content from you. And with that value comes

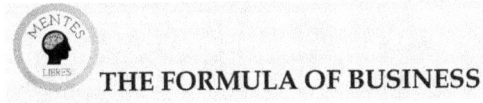

THE FORMULA OF BUSINESS

the opportunity to take your customer to the next level, where you can sell them higher quality products.

And this is not a one-sided benefit. Both you and your customer benefit from this relationship. Your customer benefits when they get even more value... something they really want. You're helping him in that regard.

And, of course, you also benefit by slowly grading your customer to your "A" list, where you can provide even more value.

I once knew a salesman from a large personnel management company. This company sold expensive computer systems that helped call centers predict the volume of

THE FORMULA OF BUSINESS

incoming calls, determine how many customer service people needed to handle those calls, and even generate the most efficient schedules for those representatives in order to maintain the desired level of service.

This guy was an old professional when it came to managing his contacts. When a potential client company made a request for proposal (basically an opportunity for your company to provide a quote based on the needs of the issuing company), they kept a record of all the people involved in the decision-making process, as well as all the support staff. Basically, the information of anyone who might have it in their hands.

Now, when he learned that a key person was moving from one company to another (which

THE FORMULA OF BUSINESS

was quite common), and that a new company was in the market for his product, he personally contacted his "leader" of the old company (who now works for the new one) and continued his funnel efforts there, while keeping the funnel in the old company.

Now imagine he was doing this for all his clues, wherever they ended up. He had funnels everywhere. Do you think he had skinny kids?

Personally I think every sale he made was well deserved. Anyone who can keep track of all those funnels and the people who jump the companies deserves to make a profit.

Figures 2-1 and 2-2 show the typical marketing funnel. Figure 2-1 shows an offline version of the funnel model, and Figure 2-2 shows the online equivalent. Note that the only differences are at the top of the funnel, which means the way you get your clues. Online they visit your website before they provide your information and become a leader. In the offline world, they would receive your offer in some other way.

A truer representation might represent your target market as suspects, who become potential customers only after you raise your hand (that is, they become your potential customers when they become your potential customers), but regardless of how you see them, the goal is to get potential customers, where you will try to turn them into potential paying customers.

Notice how the width of the funnel gets

THE FORMULA OF BUSINESS

smaller downwards? The width represents the number of customers at that height, or stage, of the funnel. However, the smaller the width, the more money they spend with you. In fact, you might think that the amount of money they spend with you is inversely proportional to the width of the funnel (more or less). So 20 percent responsible for 80 percent of their profits is at the bottom of the funnel. The other 80 percent that gives you 20 percent of your profits is towards the top. This distribution is a general observation and not a mathematical absolute. As I mentioned earlier, it can be 70/30 or 90/10 or something in between.

This is not an accident. Your "A" customers, your biggest advocates, are in the smallest segment of your customer base... the bottom of the funnel (but the top in terms of the value you deliver to them).

THE FORMULA OF BUSINESS

Figure 2-1

The marketing funnel (OFF LINE)

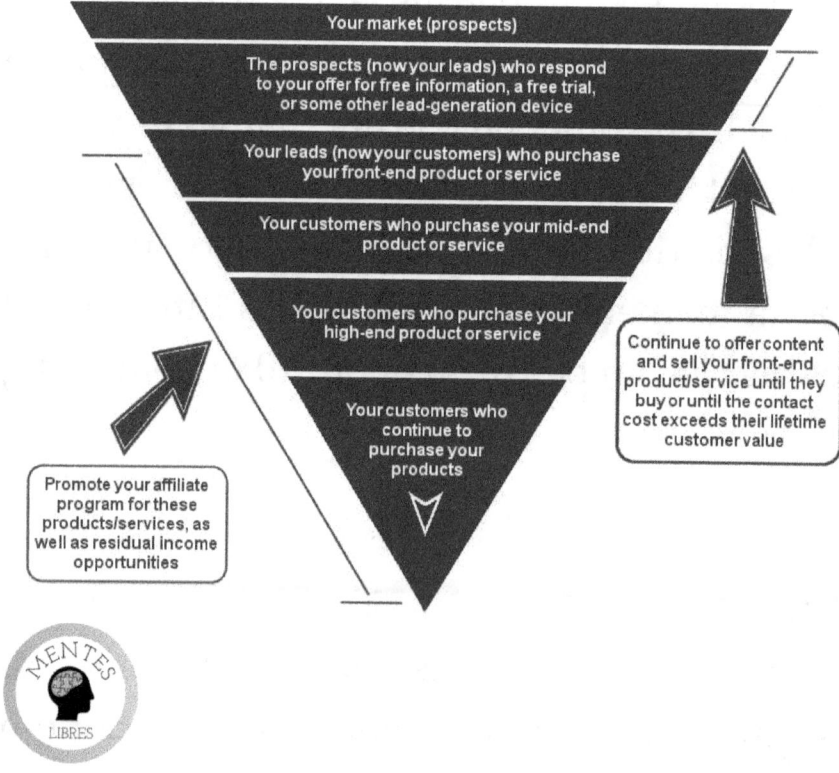

THE FORMULA OF BUSINESS

Figure 2-2

The marketing funnel (ON LINE)

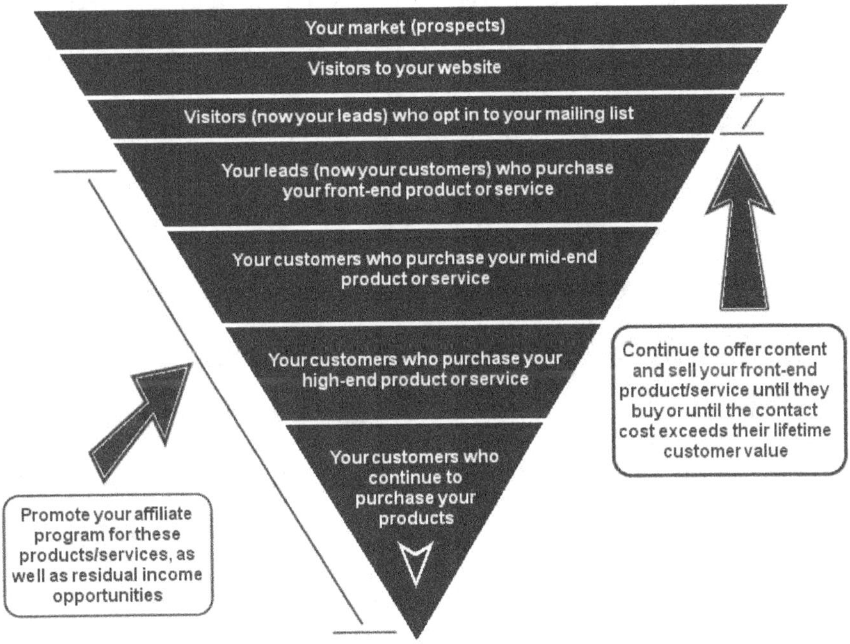

THE FORMULA OF BUSINESS

Let's walk through each step of the funnel to get a clearer understanding of how the funnel works.

1) Your prospect enters the funnel responding to your incentive or "ethical bribe" to raise your hand and give you your contact information. He is now a leader on your mailing list.

2) You continue to give him value, but you want him to make the transition from a potential customer who doesn't pay to a paying customer. As a result, you give him an initial, or entry-level, offer on a product or service directly related to the value you received when you chose to join his list. You can make the offer at a break-even point or even an initial loss, because you know you'll more than make up for it with back-end

THE FORMULA OF BUSINESS

sales.

3) If he doesn't buy your front-end product, you continue to sell it at the same offer or at different front-end offers, ideally both, because you may not be in the market for your initial offer at this time, but it may be later.

4) When you buy your front-end product, you are now a customer. Now you're "warming it up" to do more business with your company. Once you see that you fulfill your value promise, you'll feel more comfortable buying from it again.

5) You want him to move to the next price level, so make him an offer on a high-end product or service related to the entry level

THE FORMULA OF BUSINESS

he has already purchased. If he doesn't buy, you follow an approach similar to step 3 above. That is, you continue to make offers to him, but this time on the mid-level product.

6) Once he buys your mid-level product, you move on to the high-end product. Now you are conditioned to buy with confidence and without worries, because you know the exceptional value you have given it. He has seen the results of your products first hand, so your buyer's resistance is reduced. Now he's on his way to becoming one of his "A" customers, 20 percent responsible for 80 percent of his profits.

7) You continue to sell him higher ticket items and provide him with even greater value. The steps I've listed are a very simplified approach. You'll soon see that

THE FORMULA OF BUSINESS

there is a lot more if you really want to succeed in the long run, but it's not the science of long-range rockets.

After you buy, you'll want to ask for references, a testimony, and do everything in your power to make sure you're satisfied. You want you to be satisfied, so you will buy again, of course, but you also want to reduce the refund rate and get your approval. You want me to tell all your friends and colleagues about your positive experience with your company.

You probably know that when someone has a bad experience with a company, they are more likely to tell others than when they have a pleasant experience. You want to encourage them to tell all about their pleasant experience.

THE FORMULA OF BUSINESS

And then you'll want to develop some kind of residual income, where you get paid as much as a month or a year forever until it's paid off. Not everyone will, of course, but your "A" clients probably will. And you can create different residual levels, just like you have different product levels, all at different price levels.

Conclusion

This report only illustrates the types of transactions you should be thinking about for your company. In the long run, you're going to need a plan that holds your business for a longer period of time, rather than a week-to-week, month-to-month approach.

That's the real secret to building long-term success in business construction.

Exercises, such as wondering where you'd like to see your business two years from now or five years from now or ten years from now, can really make a difference in whether your business will be a short-term success

THE FORMULA OF BUSINESS

overnight that will fail quickly, or whether it will sustain the test of time and provide lifetime value for you and your family.

Ideally, you'll like to plan for the latter. And this report has barely scratched the surface.

But it does give you something to think about, because most entrepreneurs focus on the short term rather than looking at the big picture that will last a lifetime.

Visit our author page on Amazon and get more MENTES LIBRES!

http://amazon.com/author/menteslibres

If you wish, you can leave a comment on this book by clicking on the following link so that we can continue to grow! Thank you very much for your purchase!

https://www.amazon.com/dp/B0828526BR

www.ingramcontent.com/pod-product-compliance
Lightning Source LLC
Chambersburg PA
CBHW070839220526
45466CB00002B/833